THE DEATH
PENALTY

Essential Viewpoints

THE DEATH PENALTY

BY IDA WALKER

Content Consultant
Brian Bix, Ph.D.
Professor of Law and Philosophy
University of Minnesota

ABDO
Publishing Company

CREDITS

Published by ABDO Publishing Company, 8000 West 78th Street, Edina, Minnesota 55439. Copyright © 2008 by Abdo Consulting Group, Inc. International copyrights reserved in all countries. No part of this book may be reproduced in any form without written permission from the publisher. The Essential Library™ is a trademark and logo of ABDO Publishing Company.

Printed in the United States.

Editor: Jill Sherman
Copy Editor: Paula Lewis
Interior Design and Production: Nicole Brecke
Cover Design: Nicole Brecke

Library of Congress Cataloging-in-Publication Data
Walker, Ida.
  The death penalty / Ida Walker.
    p. cm. — (Essential viewpoints)
  Includes bibliographical references and index.
  ISBN 978-1-60453-055-1
  1. Capital punishment. 2. Capital punishment—Moral and ethical aspects. I. Title.

  HV8694.W35 2008
  364.66—dc22

                                    2007031915

TABLE OF CONTENTS

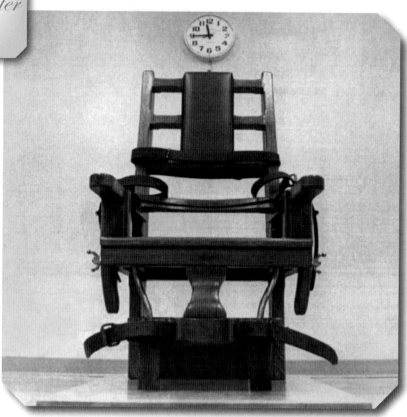

Electric chair used for executions

THE DEATH PENALTY: A SOLUTION?

In the centuries following the founding of the United States of America, the death penalty was used in many states. However, beginning in the 1960s, the U.S. Supreme Court began looking at the laws surrounding its use. The

Fifth Amendment, the Eighth Amendment, and the Fourteenth Amendment of the Constitution were considered in various cases that appeared before the Court. In some cases, the use of the death penalty was considered unconstitutional. In 1972, the Court issued a ruling that stopped the death sentence in its tracks.

In 1972, three cases sought to be heard before the Supreme Court on issues surrounding the death penalty: *Furman v. Georgia, Jackson v. Georgia*, and *Branch v. Texas*. *Furman* was a murder case. The other two cases involved rape. The Court decided the issues under review were similar and combined all three under *Furman v. Georgia*.

Twenty-six-year-old William Henry Furman was interrupted while burglarizing a home in Georgia. Furman said of the incident,

> *They got me charged with murder and I admit ... going to these folks' home and they did caught me in there and I was coming back out, backing up and there was a wire down there on the floor. I was coming out backwards and fell back and I didn't intend to kill nobody. I*

The Eighth Amendment

The Eighth Amendment has often been used in arguments opposing the death penalty. It was the basis on which the U.S. Supreme Court based its *Furman v. Georgia* ruling. The amendment states, "Excessive bail shall not be required, nor excessive fines imposed, nor cruel and unusual punishments be inflicted."[1]

The Fourteenth Amendment

In its decision to strike down some parts of the death penalty, the U.S. Supreme Court cited the first section of the Fourteenth Amendment, which states, "All persons born or naturalized in the United States, and subject to the jurisdiction thereof, are citizens of the United States and of the State wherein they reside. No State shall make or enforce any law which shall abridge the privileges or immunities of citizens of the United States; nor shall any State deprive any person of life, liberty, or property, without due process of law; nor deny to any person within its jurisdiction the equal protection of the laws."[3]

didn't know they was behind the door. The gun went off and I didn't know nothing about no murder until they arrested me.[2]

There was no question that Furman was responsible—intentionally or not—for the death of one of the home's residents. In just over 90 minutes, the jury found Furman guilty of murder. He was sentenced to death.

The other two cases were rape cases. Both of those defendants were sentenced to death as well. The three defendants whose cases challenged the death penalty were all black, poor, and lacked education. In the *Branch v. Texas* case, the defendant was also declared to be borderline mentally deficient. The justices had to consider how bias factored into the sentences of these cases. Would the imposition and carrying out of the death penalty in these three cases constitute cruel and unusual punishment in violation of the Eighth and Fourteenth Amendments?

Capital Punishment

In the legal world, there are two types of crimes: misdemeanors and felonies. Misdemeanors are less serious crimes, such as petty theft or vandalism. Punishments for these crimes likely include fines or community service. Felonies are more serious crimes, such as murder, rape, or kidnapping. Individuals convicted of committing felonies can be punished with fines and community service, but more often they are sentenced to jail or prison time—sometimes for the rest of their lives.

The death penalty is reserved for certain severe crimes, or capital crimes. The death penalty is sometimes called capital punishment. At some point in their history, most civilizations have used execution as a method of punishment. Though most of the crimes leading to execution involved murder, some nations have used (and some continue to use) the death penalty to punish crimes such as rape, treason, trafficking of humans or drugs, and even for renouncing one's religion.

Recently, there has been a worldwide trend toward abolishing the death penalty. Even in some countries where there has been no move to completely do away with the use of the death penalty, actions have been taken to limit its use. The United States is one country where use of the death penalty has been highly controversial and greatly debated.

The Heart of the Controversy

There is no question that the death penalty works as a method of punishment. The finality of capital punishment makes it impossible for the criminal to commit another crime. However, the question does arise about crime prevention. Is the death penalty the best way to prevent crime? Though it stops one criminal, does the possibility of being sentenced and put to death keep others who are considering committing a similar crime from actually committing it? The role of a sentence is also under debate. Is it meant to be rehabilitation or revenge?

Proponents and opponents of the death penalty share a desire to punish criminal behavior and protect society. The two groups' beliefs diverge in how those tasks are accomplished and whether the death penalty should be an option.

Proponents of the death penalty believe it is an effective way to stop crime. They focus on the death penalty as a deterrent, something that will stop or lessen crime. If the death penalty is a possible consequence, people will think twice about committing a crime that could lead to the death penalty. Many proponents also believe that the death penalty brings the most justice to the victim of a heinous crime.

Opponents of the death penalty believe it has proven to be an ineffective way to stop crime. They also express concern about the fairness of the giving and carrying out of a capital sentence. Opponents of the death penalty believe there are better ways to punish crime and keep society safe.

The Death Penalty in the United States

The concept of capital punishment was brought to America with the British settlers. The first execution in America occurred in Jamestown in 1608, when Captain George Kendall was executed for being a spy.

Four years after Captain Kendall's execution, Virginia's governor signed a law indicating the crimes suitable for execution. They included trading with the Native Americans, stealing fruit, and killing chickens.

In the New York colony, disrespecting one's parents and religion could result in hanging from a noose. Hitting one's parents or denying the "one true God" were offenses that called for the death penalty.

Not everyone in colonial America favored the death penalty, at least in the way it was used. Dr. Benjamin Rush, a medical pioneer and a signer of the Declaration of Independence, did not believe the death penalty turned people away from crime. He believed the opposite was true—the death penalty created more criminal behavior. Rush played an important role in the reform of Pennsylvania's capital punishment laws; by 1794, first-degree murder (pre-meditated murder) was the only crime for which someone could receive a death sentence.

The Question before the Court

According to papers filed by the attorneys of the defendants in *Furman v. Georgia*, the death sentence was unconstitutional. There had been no standard guidelines regarding which crimes would receive a death sentence. Defendants who were poor, a member of a minority group, uneducated, or mentally ill received the death penalty more often than those who did not fit these characteristics.

On June 29, 1972, by a vote of 8–1, the Supreme Court agreed with the defendants and their legal counsels. According to Justice Potter Stewart, who sided with the majority,

> These death sentences are cruel and unusual in the same way that being struck by lightning is cruel and unusual. For, of all the people convicted of rapes and murders in 1967 and 1968, many just as reprehensible as these, the petitioners are among a capriciously [unpredictably] selected random handful upon whom the sentence of death has in fact been imposed. ... If any basis can be discerned for the selection of these few to be sentenced to death, it is the constitutionally impermissible basis of race. ... I simply conclude that the Eighth and Fourteenth Amendments cannot tolerate the infliction of a sentence of death under legal systems that

permit this unique penalty to be so wantonly and freakishly imposed.[4]

REACTION TO THE RULING

Although the Court had ruled only on the conditions under which the death penalty was to be imposed, it was a powerful ruling that stopped executions for a time. Opponents of the death penalty, including the American Civil Liberties Union (ACLU), saw the ruling as an opportunity to strengthen its campaign for the abolition of the death penalty. Their goal was to take advantage of this ruling to encourage states to reevaluate their position on the issue.

Those in favor of the death penalty also went to work, helping their legislatures craft laws that addressed the concerns (that is, race bias) Justice Stewart had spelled out in his writing in support of the

Furman v. Georgia Ruling

In 1972, Supreme Court Justice William J. Brennan agreed with the majority in the *Furman v. Georgia* ruling. He wrote, in part, "Death is truly an awesome punishment. The calculated killing of a human being by the State involves, by its very nature, a denial of the executed person's humanity. ... As one 19th century proponent of punishing criminals by death declared, 'When a man is hung, there is an end of our relations with him. His execution is a way of saying, "You are not fit for this world, take your chance elsewhere."'"[5]

The First Reformer

According to historians, the first person who tried to restrict the use of the death penalty in the United States was Thomas Jefferson of the Virginia Colony. Jefferson put before the House of Burgesses, Virginia's ruling body, a bill that would limit the use of capital punishment to those who committed murder or treason. The bill lost by one vote.

Court's decision. By 1976, new death penalty laws had passed in 37 states.

In 1976, the death penalty again appeared before the U.S. Supreme Court in the case of *Gregg v. Georgia*. This time, the Court found that there were ways to improve the fairness of death penalty sentencing.

The Court determined that sentencing in capital trials would be fairer if trials were divided into the liability phase (guilty or not guilty) and the sentencing phase (years in prison, life sentences, or death penalty). According to the Court, constitutional death sentence guidelines should include objective criteria to direct and limit the sentencing, a review by an appeals court, and a consideration of the defendant's character and record. The *Gregg v. Georgia* ruling again made the death penalty a sentencing option in most states. The issue of the death penalty returned to the center of debate. ⌐

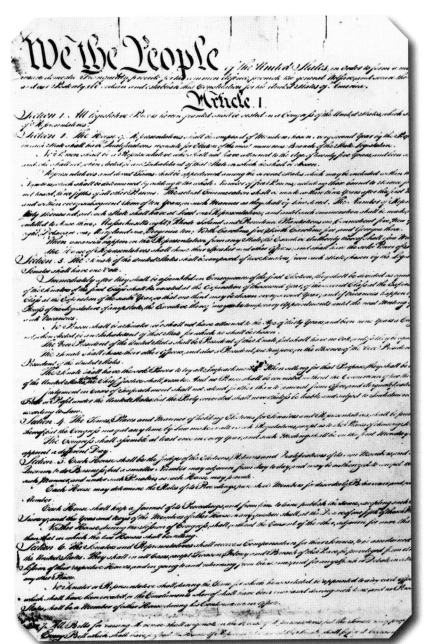

People argue about the constitutionality of the death penalty.

Decisions about the death penalty are made in courts.

Death Penalty Basics

After the U.S. Supreme Court's *Gregg v. Georgia* ruling in 1976, the path was cleared for resumption of executions for certain crimes. The death penalty was allowed in federal and military cases. Whether states wanted to make the penalty available was left to the individual legislatures.

The States and the Death Penalty

As of March 15, 2007, the death penalty was allowed in 38 states. The only states without the death penalty as a sentencing option are Alaska, Hawaii, Iowa, Maine, Massachusetts, Michigan, Minnesota, New York, North Dakota, Rhode Island, Vermont, West Virginia, and Wisconsin, along with the District of Columbia. The U.S. territories of American Samoa, Guam, Northern Mariana Islands, Puerto Rico, and the U.S. Virgin Islands also do not have the death penalty.

The Death Penalty Information Center reports that, as of September 2007, there have been 1,099 executions in the United States since the reestablishment of the death penalty in 1976. Texas leads all states in the number of executions, with 405. Since 1976, more than 80 percent of all executions have taken place in the South. Four states—Kansas, New Hampshire, New Jersey, and South Dakota—along with the U.S. military have the death penalty as a sentencing option but have not executed anyone since 1976.

Execution by the U.S. Government

In federal cases calling for the death penalty, inmates are executed by whatever method is used in the state in which the crime occurred. If the state is one that does not have the death penalty, the judge is free to choose a method used by any other state. For executions of violators of the Drug Kingpin Law, which expanded the death penalty to include murder resulting from large-scale illegal drug dealing, lethal injection is used, regardless of where the conviction took place.

More than 3,000 individuals remain on death row across the United States as of October 2007. The Death Penalty Information Center reports that California has the most inmates on death row with 660 awaiting execution. Florida follows with 397 inmates on death row, and Texas has 393.

CAPITAL PUNISHMENT CRIMES

When capital punishment first began in the United States, offenses such as stealing a chicken could bring a death sentence. The death penalty is not handed down so easily in modern times. For example, in 1977, the U.S. Supreme Court case of *Coker v. Georgia* raised the question regarding the circumstances in which the death penalty could be constituted as a cruel and unusual punishment.

Anthony Coker, who was serving a sentence for capital crimes, escaped from prison. While evading capture, he raped a woman and stole her family's car. In the trial following his recapture, Coker was found guilty and sentenced to death for the rape. The jury believed he should receive the death penalty because the rape was committed by a repeat capital offender and occurred in connection with another capital crime—armed robbery.

The case was appealed to the Georgia Supreme Court, which upheld the sentence. When it was appealed to the U.S. Supreme Court, the justices' interpretation was different. They struck down the use of the death penalty in the *Coker* case. The Court ruled that issuing the death penalty for a case in which the victim did not die was cruel and unusual punishment, a violation of the Eighth Amendment.

As a result of the U.S. Supreme Court ruling, states had to reexamine the types of crimes for which the death penalty was a sentencing option. In the past, some states allowed the death penalty for crimes such as rape, criminal assault, kidnapping, forgery, concealing the death or birth of an infant, and arson. Each state that has the death penalty allows its use in first-degree murder cases, though some require that an aggravating factor also be in place. Some states, such as California, call these factors special circumstances. For example, these factors could include the murder of a peace officer or the murder of a witness to prevent that person from testifying in court. Crimes such as treason and espionage can bring the death penalty in some states. However, in almost every state with the death penalty, the crime must have led to the death of another individual. Since 1964, only one person has been executed for a crime other than murder. As of 2007, one person was sitting on death row for a crime other than murder. He was issued the death sentence for the aggravated rape of his eight-year-old daughter.

The federal government and the U.S. military can also request the death penalty for individuals convicted of crimes within their jurisdictions. In addition to murder, crimes such as treason and espionage can be punished by death in federal and military courts.

THE PROCESS

Like all defendants in criminal cases, individuals charged with a capital crime can choose to plead guilty or not guilty. If the defendant pleads not guilty, the case will go to trial. Before each trial, in a process called *voir dire*, the defense and prosecuting attorneys question each potential juror about issues that might arise during the trial. This process helps the attorneys select an impartial jury. Personal experiences, such as being robbed, can affect a juror's feelings about a case that involved robbery. It is important to select jurors who can make a decision based solely on the facts presented in the courtroom.

The lawyers, and sometimes the trial judge, will ask the potential juror if it is possible to put aside any feelings connected with the experience and reach an unprejudiced verdict in the case on trial. If the potential juror says no or cannot convince the attorneys of his or her impartiality, the juror is excused.

When the punishment potentially involves the death penalty, the court must select a death-qualified jury. Potential jurors are asked about their feelings regarding the death penalty: Are they in favor

Arguing before the Supreme Court

Not all lawyers can argue a case before the U.S. Supreme Court. According to the Rules of the Supreme Court of the United States (2005), in order to argue a case before the Court a lawyer must:

- submit an application;
- pay a fee;
- have been admitted to law practice for three years and have not been subject to disciplinary action during that period;
- present a personal statement and references from upstanding members of the American Bar Association; and
- demonstrate that he or she possesses the qualifications necessary to argue before the U.S. Supreme Court.

of it in general? Do they feel it should be used only for certain crimes? Are they opposed to the death penalty in all cases? If the defendant is found guilty, do they feel they can recommend the death penalty?

For many people, these are not easy questions to answer. The prosecuting attorney might ask that a potential juror be excused if he or she has a limited view of the death penalty's scope. Because many people have mixed feelings about the death penalty, jury selection process for a capital punishment case can take much longer than for a trial in which the death penalty is not an option.

Even after a death sentence has been handed down, the legal process is not over. In almost every jurisdiction, the death penalty leads to an automatic appeal. Generally, appeals are restricted to questions regarding procedure, not issues of fact. For example, someone can appeal on the question of whether a particular witness should have been allowed to testify. However in most cases, the credibility of a witness's testimony cannot be argued before an appeals court. In capital punishment cases, the appeals process can take years and make its way to the U.S. Supreme Court. The inmate can ask the state governor or a pardon committee to commute the sentence, changing a sentence of death to a sentence of prison time. If none of the appeals are granted, the individual will eventually run out of items to appeal and the death sentence can be carried out.

CARRYING OUT THE DEATH PENALTY

In the United States, there are five methods of execution: lethal injection, electrocution, gas chamber, hanging, and firing squad. Most states, and the U.S. government and military, use lethal injection as either the primary or alternative method of carrying out the punishment. According to the Death Penalty Information Center, 929 inmates have been put to death by lethal injection since 1976.

An inmate facing lethal injection is brought into the execution chamber and is strapped to a gurney or a bed. The inmate is hooked up to an intravenous (IV) line to administer the drugs. Though some prisons use machines to deliver the drugs, many prisons have someone deliver the drugs manually.

By Invitation Only

Executions are private. Select members of the press, family members, close friends of the victim and the offender, attorneys, and religious counsels are often among those invited to witness the execution. The last public execution was the hanging of Rainey Bethea on August 14, 1936, in Owensboro, Kentucky. Some experts believe that a return to public executions (or even ones offered as pay-per-view events) may act as a deterrent to potential criminals.

Lethal injection usually involves three drugs. The first drug that is administered is an anesthetic, sodium thiopental. This drug causes the inmate to go into a deep sleep within approximately 30 seconds. The IV line is then flushed with a salt solution before pancuronium bromide is administered. This drug is a muscle relaxant, and it paralyzes the diaphragm and lungs, making it impossible for the inmate to breathe. This can take up to three minutes to be effective. Some states follow this drug with potassium chloride—a toxic agent. Potassium chloride prevents the heart from beating properly. Just a minute or two after the last drug is administered, medical personnel pronounce the inmate deceased. In total, the entire process usually takes between five and eighteen minutes.

The Supreme Court and state legislatures across the country have worked for many years to create a death penalty that fairly provides the punishment some feel is necessary. Despite their efforts, the death penalty is a controversial issue.

A More Humane Execution

In 1924, Nevada began using cyanide gas to execute their inmates on death row. The first inmate selected to die by gas was Gee Jon. One night as he slept in his cell, executioners tried to pump gas into his cell, hoping to carry out the death sentence while the inmate slept. The attempt was unsuccessful, and the gas chamber was invented.

The U.S. Supreme Court makes major decisions
regarding the use of the death penalty.

Demonstrators protest the death penalty.

OVERVIEW OF THE
CONTROVERSY

ew issues generate such passionate
arguments as the use of the death penalty.
People have debated its use for decades. Those
opposed feel that the punishment is too harsh.
Those in favor believe that the death penalty is

justified for violent crimes. However, it is difficult to find middle ground on the issue of life and death.

OPPOSED: THE DEATH PENALTY IS IRREVERSIBLE

When the death penalty is carried out, there is no way to undo the sentence should new evidence prove the person's innocence. Many people have been found guilty and have received the death sentence prior to use of DNA (deoxyribonucleic acid) evidence. According to the Innocence Project, a nationwide group that takes on cases in which DNA can be used to disprove guilt, 208 inmates have had their convictions overturned based on DNA evidence.

Death penalty opponents state that mandatory lifetime imprisonment does the same thing that capital punishment does—it takes criminals out of society and they no longer are a threat to public safety. A prison sentence means that the inmate can be freed, should new evidence prove that he or she is innocent.

Not a New Concept

Attempts to abolish the death penalty have occurred throughout history and across the globe. On September 15, 1848, in France, author Victor Hugo addressed the Constituent Assembly: "I have examined the death penalty under each of its two aspects: as a direct action, and as an indirect one. What does it come down to? Nothing but something horrible and useless, nothing but a way of shedding blood that is called a crime when an individual commits it, but is (sadly) called 'justice' when society brings it about ..."[1]

Opposed: The Death Penalty Is Issued Unfairly

For a punishment to be just, it must be issued fairly. Opponents of the death penalty cite numerous studies that show that the poor and members of a minority group, especially African Americans, are more likely to receive the death penalty than are white, more affluent defendants convicted of the same crime.

In 1999, the American Bar Association (ABA), a national organization representing more than 400,000 attorneys across the United States, called for a halt on executions because the death sentence was not handed out fairly. In 2000, Illinois Governor George Ryan placed a moratorium on executions after misconduct was found. Since 1977, 13 inmates in Illinois on death row have been cleared of murder charges while awaiting execution; 12 inmates have been executed during the same time frame. Ryan believed there was a flaw in the system because so many people who were sentenced to capital punishment were cleared of the charges. Before leaving office, Ryan commuted the sentences of 167 inmates to life without parole or lesser sentences and pardoned four inmates.

In 2002, Maryland Governor Paris Glendening halted executions because of unfairness. Also in 2002, New Mexico Governor Gary Johnson declared his state's death penalty unfair, claiming it risked the execution of innocent individuals.

OPPOSED: THE DEATH PENALTY SOLVES NOTHING

According to opponents of the death penalty, nothing is gained by executing an inmate. They admit that it does take one criminal off the streets, but just one. Opponents cite Federal Bureau of Investigation (FBI) statistics that seem to support their position that capital punishment does not work as a deterrent to lower the murder rate. According to the FBI's 2005 report, murder rates were highest in the South and the West. Those are also the regions with the highest execution rates and the most inmates sitting on death row.

Premeditation

According to the Ontario Consultants on Religious Tolerance, murders are seldom premeditated. Instead, they are committed for many reasons or by individuals for whom the death penalty does not factor in as a deterrent. The Ontario Consultants state that most murders are committed:

- during domestic disputes and are not premeditated;
- under the influence of alcohol or drugs when the individual is in an altered state;
- by hit men, who do not expect to be caught;
- by psychopaths or mentally ill individuals who are unable to understand right and wrong or have altered views on human life;
- by self-destructive individuals who want to die; and
- by brain-damaged individuals who may be unable to control their emotions.

Opponents of the death penalty also point to the reasons murders are committed. According to death penalty opponents, most murders are not premeditated. Rather, they are spur-of-the-moment occurrences, committed in rage or under the influence of some substance. According to former Texas Attorney General Jim Mattox, under whose administration many executions were carried out:

> *It is my own experience that those executed in Texas were not deterred by the existence of the death penalty law. I think in most cases you'll find that the murder was committed under severe drug and alcohol abuse.* [2]

In addition, a death penalty sentence costs the state more money than it would to keep the individual in prison for life. The costs of the trial and appeal process for a death penalty case are much higher than other cases. Jury selection for death penalty cases often takes longer than for trials where the death penalty is not an issue. That means salaries of court staff and attorneys, as well as utility and incidental costs, are higher for a death penalty case. The appeals process for a death sentence can take years; inmates have spent as long as 20 years on death row filing appeals and delaying their executions. Each step of the process adds to the cost of the death penalty.

In Favor: The Death Penalty Takes Dangerous Criminals off the Streets

According to proponents of the death penalty, one can never be certain that anything less than a death sentence can ensure that a dangerous criminal will not be allowed back into society. They point to the fact that a life sentence does not always mean the inmate will be locked up

The Innocence Project

In 1992, two civil rights attorneys, Peter Neufeld and Barry Scheck, established the Innocence Project at the Benjamin N. Cardoza School of Law in New York City. The project uses post-conviction DNA evidence to help free inmates who have been unjustly convicted and incarcerated. Many people in jail today were convicted of crimes before DNA testing was available. DNA of blood, hair, or other bodily fluids left at a crime scene can be compared to the defendant's. If the DNA does not match, it means someone else was at the crime scene.

The project receives thousands of requests for help from inmates, inmates' families, and defense attorneys all over the country. Law students and other volunteers examine the case file, checking to see if DNA could possibly free the inmate. They also have to find out if there is any DNA evidence to test. Sometimes it is impossible for the Innocence Project to take on the case because there is no such evidence. Other times, the project takes on a client, discovers that he is innocent, and the inmate is freed. On occasion, DNA testing by the Innocence Project proves that an inmate who claims to be innocent is in fact, guilty.

The success of the original Innocence Project has spawned other such projects across the country, all working together to use science to free wrongly convicted individuals.

Tiffany Reising speaks to reporters following the execution of her mother's murderer.

for the rest of his or her life. Life sentences can be commuted to a specific number of years. With time off for good behavior, inmates, even dangerous ones, sometimes can be released from prison after serving just a fraction of their sentence.

In recent years, more dangerous criminals have been released because of prison overcrowding. Because prisons are unable to fulfill a life sentence, many dangerous criminals are allowed back into society.

In Favor: The Death Penalty Provides Closure for the Victim's Family

Victims' families often desire a death sentence to provide closure to the tragic event. According to proponents, a death sentence and execution can help those who have lost a loved one move past the tragedy that often consumes their lives.

Proponents believe that sentencing a defendant to life in prison does not have the same healing effects for the victim's family as putting the individual to death. There is always the possibility in the back of their minds that the inmate may one day be released or escape and commit more crimes.

Even a mandatory life sentence does not offer families the relief of the death penalty. While their loved one will never see another day, the inmate will. Though incarcerated, the inmate is still alive and able to

Victims Against the Death Penalty

Not every family that has experienced the loss of a loved one through a violent act looks to the death penalty as a way to find closure. Some families join together to work toward an end to the death penalty.

The Murder Victims' Families for Human Rights (MVFHR) is a group that works to oppose all forms of the death penalty worldwide. The Murder Victims' Families for Reconciliation (MVFR) provides speakers and educational programs concentrating on the reform of the criminal justice system.

Members of the Journey of Hope travel all over the country, telling their individual stories of how the death penalty affected their lives.

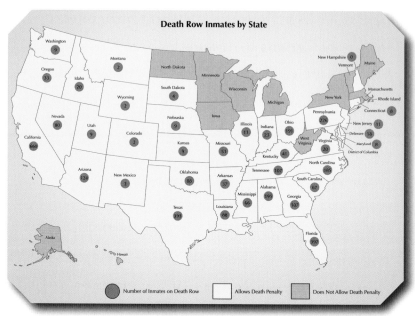

As of January 1, 2007, there were 3,350 inmates on death row.

have a relationship with friends and family. The
same cannot be said for the victim.

In Favor: The Death Penalty Can Prevent
Future Crimes

Proponents of the death penalty often cite the
punishment's effectiveness as a deterrent to others
contemplating the commission of a capital crime
such as murder. The possibility of receiving the
death penalty may stop someone from committing

a murder. To support the argument, proponents cite a controversial 1973 study by Isaac Ehrlich. For several years, criminologists had been studying the relationship between murder rates and the death penalty, but they had been unable to come up with any conclusions. Using Ehrlich's analysis, it was determined that for every inmate who received the death penalty and was executed, seven individuals turned away from committing murder. Ehrlich's study has been contested by other researchers.

Another person who has studied the effect of capital punishment on murder rates is Professor Ernest van den Haag, a professor of Jurisprudence and Public Policy at Fordham University. Van den Haag was a vocal proponent of the death penalty until his death in 2002. His report states that:

> *capital punishment is likely to deter more than other punishments because people fear death more than anything else. They fear most death deliberately inflicted by law and scheduled by courts. Whatever people fear most is likely to deter most. Hence, the threat of the death penalty may deter some murderers who otherwise might not have been deterred.*[3]

But proponents of the death penalty do not limit the deterrent effects to those outside of prison. The safety of guards and law enforcement personnel are also benefits of the death penalty. When someone is serving a maximum sentence of life in prison—even without the possibility of parole—there is little to prevent the inmate from killing a guard or other inmate. ⌐

A family calls for the execution of a murderer.

Sentences of stoning and execution in Bauchi, Nigeria,
are imposed under Islamic law.

RELIGION AND DEATH
PENALTY PROPONENTS

The United States was founded by individuals
escaping religious persecution in their
homeland. Religion played an important role in
the beginning of the nation, and it continues to be
a major force on the political scene—including the

issue of the death penalty. However, religion is not as important to some people as it is to others. The U.S. Constitution guarantees the right to practice religion freely. By extension, it also guarantees one's right not to practice any religion.

RELIGION AND THE DEATH PENALTY: AN OVERVIEW

Just like one's decision to practice—or not practice—a particular religious belief, choice also plays a part in an individual's position on the death penalty. For some people, particular spiritual beliefs may have a strong influence on how they feel about the death penalty. Studies have found, however, that religious belief does not always go hand in hand with a person's position on the death penalty. According to the Ontario Consultants on Religious Tolerance, those individuals within a denomination often support the

God's Punishment

According to the Old Testament, there were certain sins for which a trial or determination by a human jury was not required. God would impose the death penalty without the "interference" of human beings. These sins include:
- wickedness,
- being abusive to strangers,
- being excessively curious, and
- practicing birth control.

death penalty although their faith is opposed to it. According to the Ontario Consultants, only the Southern Baptist, the Lutheran Church, the Missouri Synod, and the Latter-day Saints are in favor of retaining the death penalty. Other denominations, such as Pentecostal churches and Judaism, are mixed in their views on the death penalty. Although not everyone's personal beliefs on the death penalty are in line with their religion, these religious or spiritual beliefs can play a significant part in helping individuals reach a decision regarding how they feel about the issue of the death penalty.

CHRISTIANITY: MAN IS MADE IN GOD'S IMAGE

Christianity is the dominant religion in the United States. Roman Catholic, Eastern Orthodox, Lutheran, and Protestant religions

The Separation of Church and State

The early colonists came to the shores of America largely because they had suffered religious persecution in their homeland. Many countries had a national religion. Anyone who believed differently was often treated poorly and denied many of the rights given to other citizens.

When the Founding Fathers addressed the issue of religion in the U.S. Constitution, they wanted to ensure freedom of religion. The First Amendment to the Constitution reads in part, "Congress shall make no law respecting an establishment of religion, or prohibiting the free exercise thereof."[1] U.S. citizens could choose to practice any religion they wished—or none—without fear of government interference.

Edward Kelley is in favor of execution.

are all denominations of Christianity. Christian denominations differ in some aspects of their beliefs. However, they are all founded on one major principle: Jesus Christ is the Son of God. The Bible is Christianity's holy book. It tells the story of God, creation, and the life of Jesus Christ.

Christian proponents of the death penalty generally look to the Bible for support. Genesis, the

Some death penalty opponents believe the punishment is cruel and unusual.

first book of the Bible, contains the first mention of death as an appropriate punishment for someone who had murdered another person. As written in the King James version of the Bible:

> *Whoso sheddeth man's blood, by man shall his blood be shed: for in the image of God he made man.*[2]

This passage claims that because all people were made in the image of God, such an offense was seen as being an act against God. A crime against God required the ultimate punishment.

Other books of the Bible contain references to crimes that could lead to the death penalty. According to the King James version of the Bible, other crimes punishable by death include: following another religion or trying to convince someone to change religions, trying to communicate with the dead, cursing or abusing one's parents, working on the Sabbath (holy day), practicing gluttony or drinking excessively, and committing adultery.

Some Christians believe that because the Bible indicates that there are certain offenses that should be punished by death, it justifies the continued use of the death penalty. Many Christians believe that the

Conservative Supporters

In general, the more conservative the denomination, the more likely it is to support the death penalty. Conservative religions follow their religious books closely, believing them to be the word of God and allowing for little interpretation.

Bible is truly the word of God and should be followed as closely as possible.

JUDAISM: CRIMES MUST BE WITNESSED

Judaism, the Jewish religion, shares many similarities with Christianity. The basic difference between the Jewish faith and Christianity is that the Jewish faith does not believe that Jesus was the Son of God. The Torah, the Jewish holy book, consists of the first five books of the Christian Bible. The Talmud is the book of Jewish law.

According to the official teachings of Judaism, the death penalty is an acceptable form of punishment. Because the Jewish Torah follows portions of the Christian Bible, Jewish proponents of the death penalty cite similar religious evidence that the death penalty is appropriate.

The Death Penalty in Israel

Adolf Eichmann was the only person to be executed in the State of Israel. Eichmann was the author of the "Final Solution to the Jewish Question," which detailed the Holocaust. Six million Jewish people were executed in concentration camps during World War II. After the war, Eichmann fled to Argentina. He was found by Israel's intelligence agency and returned to Israel, where he stood trial for his war crimes. Eichmann was convicted and sentenced to death by hanging.

In addition to the Torah, Judaism places a responsibility on those witnessing the crime. If the death penalty is to be imposed, it requires two witnesses (not female or close family members) who attempted to tell the offender that what he or she was doing was wrong.

ISLAM: PUNISHMENT THAT SERVES THE CRIME

Islamic law is based primarily on the teachings of the Prophet Muhammad. Followers of Islam are called Muslims. The Qur'an, Islam's holy book, is similar to the Bible and the Torah. Under Islam, there are different types of crimes. The most serious crimes, the Hudud or Hadd, are those that threaten the existence of Islam. Punishment for these crimes, which include adultery, theft, drunkenness, and rebellion, is spelled out in the Qur'an. Under the Tazir category of crimes, the death penalty can also be given.

Under Islam, there are two crimes that require the death penalty: adultery and apostasy, or the renunciation of faith. While Islam encourages restraint in issuing punishment, it also recognizes that, in addition to these, there are other cases where the death penalty would be applied.

Despite the fact that many religions appear to support the death penalty, there are many individuals within those religions with opposing views. For most people, moral beliefs are closely linked to their feelings about the death penalty. Therefore, many of those opposed to the death penalty cite religious evidence as well. ⌐

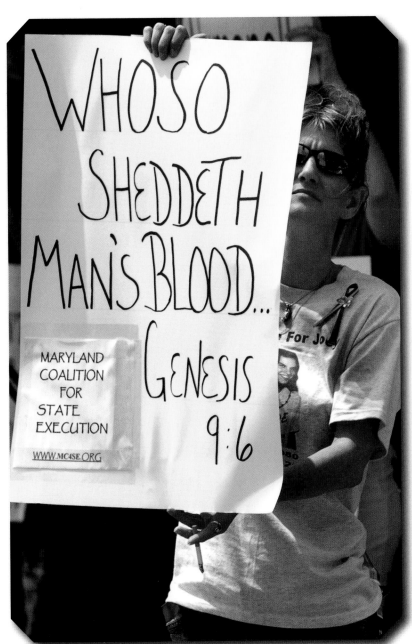

WHOSO SHEDDETH MAN'S BLOOD... GENESIS 9:6

MARYLAND COALITION FOR STATE EXECUTION

WWW.MC4SE.ORG

A death penalty proponent cites the Bible in support of her view.

Pope John Paul II strongly opposed the use of the death penalty.

RELIGION AND DEATH
PENALTY OPPONENTS

*A*lthough someone's religion may
be officially in favor of the death
penalty, personal opinions can affect an individual's
position. In addition, certain denominations of a
religion may take a more liberal stance. Individuals

may also interpret the words of their religious books differently than what is normally taught.

CHRISTIANITY: TEACHING FORGIVENESS

The Bible tells the story of two brothers, Cain and Abel. Cain killed his brother out of jealousy, and God gave Cain his punishment:

> *And now art thou cursed from the earth, which hath opened her mouth to receive thy brother's blood from thy hand ... a fugitive and a vagabond shalt thou be in the earth. ... And the Lord said unto him, Therefore whosoever slayeth Cain, vengeance shall be taken on him sevenfold. And the Lord set a mark upon Cain, lest any finding him should kill him.* [1]

Instead of sentencing Cain to death, God sent him to wander the earth. Christians who oppose the death penalty often cite this biblical story as grounds for their opposition.

The Pope

In the Catholic Church, the Pope, the highest religious leader, is believed to be infallible. This means that when he speaks on church law, he can never be wrong. Pope John Paul II was adamantly against the death penalty. Pope Benedict XVI has said that capital punishment is contrary to Christian catechism, or its body of principles. For some devout Catholics, the Pope's word is reason enough to be opposed to the death penalty.

Opponents of the death penalty also point out that Christianity is based on the teachings and life of Jesus Christ. They believe that the New Testament, the part of the Bible written after Jesus was born, should be followed more closely. There are very few references to the concept of a penalty by death in the New Testament. Instead, Jesus is depicted as showing compassion to those whose actions, under the Old Testament, would have resulted in a death sentence. Christians are encouraged to forgive rather than to seek revenge. One reason is the belief that God

Karla Faye Tucker

Some prison inmates find comfort in religion and wholeheartedly convert. In some cases, those close to these inmates claim that religion has completely changed them and that they no longer resemble the person who committed the crime. Death row has been the scene of many of these "acts of contrition."

One of the most famous inmates to seek forgiveness was Karla Faye Tucker. In 1984, she was convicted of participating in a murder and sentenced to death. During the more than ten years she spent on Texas's death row, Tucker became a born-again Christian. She counseled other inmates, and many people who knew her believed Tucker was a changed woman.

Calls came from all over the world asking then-governor George Bush to commute her sentence to life without parole. Some of those calling for her sentence to be commuted were people who had favored the death sentence for her particular crime. But because Tucker had found God, they did not see the need for her to be executed. She was a changed person, no longer a threat to society.

Governor Bush refused to commute the sentence and Karla Faye Tucker was executed by lethal injection on February 3, 1998.

Karla Faye Tucker found religion while in prison.

will forgive anyone who repents their sins: execution prevents the person from repenting.

Judaism: Restrictions Limit Use of the Death Penalty

Though the Jewish religion considers the death penalty an appropriate punishment for some crimes, it has been eliminated in the two sets of writings that make up the Talmud, the Mishnah, and the Gemara. Restrictions such as the two-witness rule have limited the use of the death penalty. According to Rabbi Aryeh Kaplan:

these punishments were almost never invoked, and existed mainly as deterrent and to indicate the seriousness of the sins for which they were prescribed. The rules of evidence and other safeguards that the Torah provides to protect the accused made it all but impossible to actually invoke these penalties. ... The system of judicial punishments could become brutal and barbaric unless administered in an atmosphere of the highest morality and piety. [2]

Longtime Opponents

The Mennonites, the Amish, the Quakers, and the Unitarian Universalists have been among the most vocal death penalty opponents since executions were first allowed in the United States.

Maimonides was a doctor, philosopher, and Jewish scholar in the Middle Ages. He wrote extensively about the death penalty and was concerned with the possibility that errors could occur when it was used. He warned, "It is better and more satisfactory to acquit a thousand guilty persons than to put a single innocent one to death."[3] During Maimonides's time, his opinions were among the minority. Today, he is considered one of the most knowledgeable and important scholars of Jewish philosophy and law.

Orthodox Judaism, one of the most conservative forms of the religion, is wary of the death penalty's use in modern society and supports the strict regulations surrounding it. Reform Judaism, one of the more liberal branches, has formally opposed the death penalty since 1959. The Union of Reform Judaism resolved, "We believe that there is no crime for which the taking of human life by society is justified, and that it is the obligation of society to evolve other methods in dealing with crime."[4]

Islam: Punishment Should Be Sympathetic and Fair

Throughout history, Islam has shown a tendency toward mercy. Like other religions, forgiveness is a major principle in Islam. In many Islamic countries, the victims' families play a major role in determining the punishment. A victim's family may choose to forgive a defendant who, instead of being put to death, will be sentenced to prison and required to pay compensation to the family. If the defendant is unable to pay the amount ordered, the state arranges for the victim's family to be compensated.

Under Islam, punishment is to be rendered fairly and with sympathy. Revenge and retaliation are not to be considered when determining the proper punishment for a crime. Those responsible for rendering a punishment should not exhibit the characteristics that might have led the guilty party to commit the crime in the first place.

Individuals and groups within a religion may still disagree with one another over issues regarding the death penalty. Religion plays a major role in many individuals' personal decisions about the issue, as well as in influencing a government's decisions on capital punishment. Still, it is not the only factor. Moral, economic, and social factors also influence personal decisions about the death penalty.

Saeed Razavi holds Iran's Constitution as he speaks to students
in opposition of the death penalty.

A jury's decision may be influenced by its bias.

OBJECTIONS TO THE DEATH PENALTY

*P*eople oppose the death penalty for many reasons. Some are against it for religious reasons, but others base their objections on moral, economic, or social grounds. There is also a body of laws that indicate what behaviors are appropriate for a particular society. These are part of what makes a society orderly.

But morals go beyond what is legal. There are times when morals and the law conflict. Opponents of the death penalty know that it is upheld by the law in certain states, but for many, it goes against their personal beliefs.

RACE AND THE DEATH PENALTY

Opponents are concerned about the role race plays in the death penalty issue. Most of the inmates awaiting execution are members of a minority group, though as of September 2007, most of those executed were white.

Those who oppose the death penalty on the basis of racial bias believe the racial imbalance of those on death row is unfair. They point to the fact that minorities are more likely to be sentenced to death for a capital crime than are white defendants. This is especially true if the victim was white. Researchers at

What Is a Stereotype?

People make judgments about other people. Sometimes those opinions come after knowing the other person for a while. Sometimes they are snap judgments based on little information concerning a person's appearance, income level, religion, or occupation. For example, the idea that all used-car salespeople lie to get people to buy their cars is a stereotype. So when a person meets one in any circumstance, he or she may think the salesperson cannot be trusted. Other stereotypes are more harmful.

Stanford University studied the relationship between black defendants and white or black victims to see if the defendant's appearance was related to a sentence of death. According to their results, the researchers found:

> *Male murderers with stereotypically "black-looking" features are more than twice as likely to get the death sentence than lighter-skinned African-American defendants provided the victim in both situations is White. … The relationship between physical appearance and the death sentence disappears, however, when both murderers and their victims are Black.* [1]

These findings indicate that jurors allow their perceptions of race to influence their decisions when deciding a verdict. Dr. Jennifer Eberhardt, one of the study's researchers, summarized the results:

> *Race clearly matters in criminal justice in ways in which people may or may not be consciously aware. When black defendants are accused of killing whites, perhaps jurors use the degree to which these defendants appear stereotypically black as a proxy for criminality, and then punish accordingly.* [2]

But according to opponents of the death penalty, race becomes a factor long before the sentencing. Minority defendants are likely to depend on a court-appointed public defender or legal aid attorney in their trials. These attorneys often have heavy caseloads, and as a result, they may not be able to devote as much time to their clients' cases as private attorneys. These kinds of lawyers also do not have the resources, such as investigators or support staff, to help prepare the case for defense.

Economic Status and the Death Penalty

According to opponents of capital punishment, those who receive the death penalty are usually defendants who cannot afford a private attorney in their defense. An effective defense is extremely expensive and requires that the attorney and staff conduct their own investigation in order to counter the prosecution's case. The cost of mounting an adequate defense is outside the capabilities of most defendants facing the death penalty. Though many public defenders and

Race and Juries

Trial attorneys have some say in the selection of the jury. They try to choose jurors who they feel will not allow race to influence their decisions. The attorneys for the defense and prosecution can reject a potential juror "for cause." When an attorney asks that a juror be rejected for cause, he or she must present a reason to the presiding judge.

The other type of challenge is called peremptory. The attorneys for the defense and prosecution each receive a certain number of peremptory challenges. For this type of challenge, lawyers do not need to provide a reason. A lawyer might reject a juror using a peremptory challenge if he or she suspects that the potential juror might not be honest about his or her feelings about an issue being dealt with in the trial.

legal aid attorneys are highly skilled and dedicated to their clients, some are not able to meet the demands of a capital punishment case. More affluent defendants can afford private attorneys, those with the time, experience, and resources necessary to mount a strong case for their client. The appeals process is very expensive as well. The poorest inmates are often unable to hire established appeals attorneys or pay for important tests and investigations.

In addition, the position of a public defender is being eliminated in many states as a cost-savings measure. In these states, defendants who cannot afford to hire their own counsel are appointed private attorneys by the state. Some question whether a private attorney will show the same dedication and apply the same amount of resources to these cases for which they are paid much less. Court-appointed defenders in Mississippi, for example, receive a flat fee of only $1,000 for such cases. The attorneys appointed for death penalty cases may not

Quality of Counsel

A study by the American Civil Liberties Union (ACLU) found that lawyers of Virginia death row inmates were six times more likely to be disciplined by the bar association than other attorneys. Lawyers for one in ten inmates in the Virginia penal system would lose their license to practice at some point during their career. The ACLU cites these findings as support that those incarcerated did not have adequate representation.

The financial ability to hire quality counsel can affect the strength of a defendant's case.

necessarily have experience in criminal cases, let alone those cases that could bring the death penalty.

Inadequate representation in death penalty cases has not gone unnoticed by the Supreme Court. In 2001, Justice Ruth Bader Ginsberg wrote that she had, *yet to see a death case among the dozens coming to the Supreme Court ... in which the defendant was well represented at trial. People who are well represented at trial do not get the death penalty.*[3]

CRUEL AND UNUSUAL PUNISHMENT

Opponents of the death penalty believe that executions violate the Eighth Amendment of the U.S. Constitution, which prohibits cruel and unusual punishment. The U.S. Supreme Court has ruled that in order for the death penalty to be in violation of the Eighth Amendment, it must be both cruel and unusual.

Death penalty opponents believe that putting someone to death for a crime is unusual. As for cruel, the methods have been revisited on occasion. In Florida, electrocutions were halted for a time when the chair, called "Old Sparky," began to do just that—spark and smoke during executions. For many years, it was said that execution by lethal injection was painless; the inmate would simply go to sleep. A study published in April 2007 indicated that some inmates had not received enough thiopental, which meant that they had likely suffered serious pain. To opponents of capital punishment, this proves that lethal injections are cruel and unusual punishment.

In September 2007, the Supreme Court agreed to hear an appeal by two men on Kentucky's death row arguing that lethal injections are cruel and unusual punishment under the Eighth Amendment. They argue that the drugs used for lethal injections paralyze the condemned while they painfully suffocate. Texas has since temporarily halted executions until the Supreme Court makes a ruling. Because lethal injection is the most widely used form of execution, the

Fear-filled Last Moments

Philip Workman was convicted on charges of killing a Memphis, Tennessee, police officer in 1982 after trying to rob a Wendy's restaurant. Workman's execution date had been scheduled four times; three times it had been legally suspended. The fourth execution date was set for May 9, 2007.

In the days leading up to his execution, Workman spoke publicly about his upcoming execution, expressing fear at the method—lethal injection. He told CNN reporter Ashley Fantz that he had heard that inmates undergoing lethal injection probably felt extreme pain before they died. He did not want to suffer. Workman's comments added fuel to the debate surrounding the use of lethal injections in executions.

Workman refused to eat his last meal. Instead, he asked that the $20 be spent on a pizza for a homeless person. Correctional facility staff refused his request, saying that they were not authorized to make charitable contributions. When that story hit the media, more than 100 pizzas, donated from all over the country, were delivered to homeless shelters and rescue missions in the state.

Philip Workman, with all of his appeals exhausted, was executed on May 9, 2007.

ruling could have a huge effect on how states will carry out the death penalty.

DEADLY MISTAKES

Opponents of the death penalty admit that there is no definitive proof that an innocent person has ever been executed. However, most believe it is only a matter of time before this occurs or before evidence comes to light to indicate that it already has.

According to the Innocence Project, 208 imprisoned individuals have been found innocent based solely on DNA evidence. Some of those people were facing execution. The Death Penalty Information Center states that between 2000 and 2004, through DNA tests and other methods, 35 inmates were proved to be innocent and released from death row. Opponents believe the risk of putting an innocent person to death should be reason enough to end the use of the death penalty.

Women on Death Row

In 1632, Jane Champion was the first woman executed in the United States. The number of women who have been executed is much lower than men, in part because women are convicted of capital crimes far less frequently. Eleven women have been executed since 1976. As of July 30, 2007, 49 women were sitting on death row.

Death penalty opponents hold a protest against its use.

Doctors and the Death Penalty

As of April 2007, death row inmates in three states had challenged the use of lethal injections. And for the first time, judges agreed that lethal injections could be a cruel and unusual punishment if a doctor was not present to make certain the inmate did not suffer. Although some doctors support the death penalty, many do not feel they can professionally participate in lethal injections.

As part of becoming a doctor, individuals take the Hippocratic Oath stating that they will abide by the principles of the medical profession. The oath reads in part:

> *Most especially must I tread with care in matters of life and death. If it is given me to save a life, all thanks. But it may also be within my power to take a life; this awesome responsibility must be faced with great humbleness and awareness of my own frailty. Above all, I must not play at God.* [4]

In North Carolina, the presence of doctors at executions is legally required. According to attorneys who argued on behalf of North Carolina death row inmates, the oath requires that doctors treat a dying inmate, thereby preventing death by execution.

Individuals opposed to the death penalty recognize that, depending on the crime, some people should be incarcerated for life. However, they do not believe the death penalty is necessary to achieve public safety or to punish dangerous criminals.

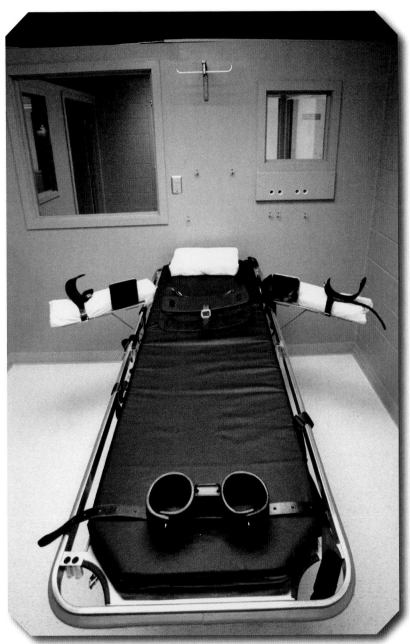

Table used to administer lethal injections

Law enforcement gather to search for Jessica Lunsford.

SUPPORT FOR THE
DEATH PENALTY

People in favor of the death penalty feel just as strongly about their opinion as those who are against it. Some proponents believe that those who oppose the death penalty care more about the perpetrator than the victims. Proponents of the death penalty state that they are on the victim's side. Those in favor of the death penalty have moral arguments on their side as well.

The Seriousness of the Crime

Nine-year-old Jessica Lunsford was discovered missing from her bedroom in the early morning of February 24, 2005. Jessica's family called the authorities, and Florida law enforcement and volunteers began searching for her immediately.

On March 17, 2005, John Evander Couey was arrested in Georgia. He had been living in Florida, near Jessica's home, at the time of her disappearance. Law enforcement discovered that Couey had kidnapped Jessica. When he became frightened that law enforcement was narrowing its search down to him, Couey put Jessica in a plastic garbage bag and buried her alive.

In March 2007, a Florida jury found Couey guilty of kidnapping and murder and recommended that he receive the death penalty.

Proponents of the death penalty point to individuals such as John

> "It is by exacting the highest penalty for the taking of human life that we affirm the highest value of human life."[1]
> —*Edward Koch, New York City mayor, 1978–1989*

Evander Couey as prime examples of why the death penalty is a good thing. Couey had a long criminal record, including previous arrests for sexual offenses against a child. Despite receiving a ten-year sentence for one crime, he had been released on parole after serving just two years. Although given a decade-long sentence, Couey served only a fraction of the time, something that proponents feel happens too often. Even with a life sentence, there is no guarantee that perpetrators will not be released from prison.

Proponents argue that some crimes are so heinous that the only appropriate

An Argument for Deterrence

Execution of those who have committed heinous murders may deter only one murder per year. If it does, it seems quite warranted. It is also the only fitting retribution for murder I can think of.

... I would favor retention of the death penalty as retribution even if it were shown that the threat of execution could not deter prospective murderers not already deterred by the threat of imprisonment. Still, I believe the death penalty, because of its finality, is more feared than imprisonment, and deters some prospective murderers not deterred by the thought of imprisonment. Sparing the lives of even a few prospective victims by deterring their murderers is more important than preserving the lives of convicted murderers because of the possibility, or even the probability, that executing them would not deter others. Whereas the life of the victims who might be saved are valuable, that of the murderer has only negative value because of his crime. Surely the criminal law is meant to protect the lives of potential victims in preference to those of actual murderers.[2]

—Ernest van der Haag, Professor of Jurisprudence and Public Policy at Fordham University, 1986 punishment is death. Some criminals have had repeated opportunities at rehabilitation but continue to return to crime. And as in the case with Couey, the crimes become progressively worse.

Most people would probably agree that violent crimes, such as the murder of a child, should be punished severely. Proponents of the death penalty believe that the way to do this is by execution. An Oklahoma district attorney describes one defendant who he believed warranted the death penalty based on his viciousness:

> In 1991, a young mother was rendered helpless and made to watch as her baby was executed. The mother was then mutilated and killed. The killer should not lie in some prison with three meals a day, clean sheets, cable TV, family visits and endless appeals. For justice to prevail, some killers just need to die.[3]

KNOWING RIGHT AND WRONG

Most people know that their actions can have consequences. A basic understanding of right and wrong is expected of most adults, as well as an understanding of the consequences. This knowledge makes a person responsible for his or her actions. A normal person who commits murder understands the seriousness of the crime and should be prepared for serious consequences.

Proponents of the death penalty often cite this argument to support the death penalty. Individuals who commit murder know they are committing a crime and should expect a serious punishment. For proponents of the death penalty, that punishment is execution.

That is not to say that proponents of the death penalty necessarily believe that everyone responsible for the death of another person deserves the death penalty. There are different degrees of responsibility attached to causing the death of another person. Death penalty proponents understand that different death-related crimes require different levels of punishment. But according to proponents, for the highest category of murder—first-degree murder— the death penalty should be an available punishment option.

Respect and Compassion for the Victim and Family

Some critics believe that in today's justice system, criminals are awarded more rights than the victim or the victim's family. Critics believe that the victim gets lost in the sea of legal motions and procedures that guarantee the defendant receives a fair trial.

Death penalty proponents want respect shown to the victim and to the victim's family and friends. Many death penalty proponents believe that the execution of the murderer shows that respect and that the victim's life had meaning and importance. In addition, many proponents of the death penalty believe that the execution of the murderer helps victims' families find closure and move on with their lives. With the execution, the family knows the person who caused them such grief will not be able to harm another family.

Proponents of the death penalty also question the more practical issues of lifetime imprisonment on victims' families. For those living in the same state as the inmate, their tax dollars go toward keeping the murderer of their loved one alive. Even for those who do not live in the same state, some of their federal tax dollars either directly or indirectly help

Only about Revenge?

When asked if the death penalty is an act of revenge, the sister-in-law of one murder victim responded, "Revenge would be going out and killing one of [the murderer's] family members ... The death penalty isn't revenge. It's the law."[4]

support the inmate. Proponents do not believe it is fair to expect the families to support the inmate.

The Expense of Execution

One of the arguments often used by opponents of the death penalty to support their position is that it is more expensive to execute an inmate than to keep the individual locked up—even for life. However, according to death penalty proponents, a large proportion of those costs is spent on the appeal process.

Proponents of the death penalty argue that the state could limit the number of times an inmate could appeal a decision. Some inmates have spent as many as 20 years on death row. Much of that time has been spent filing appeal after appeal. Proponents do not ask that the appeals process be done away with, just that it have limits.

It Is the Law

Technically, the death penalty is not part of the U.S. Constitution. Individual state legislatures enact laws that set the parameters for when the death penalty will come into play, how the execution will be carried out, and other issues concerning the punishment. When it is believed that the rules surrounding a state's death penalty might conflict with the U.S. Constitution, a case can be brought before the U.S. Supreme Court.

According to some proponents, the justice system is morally obligated to make the death penalty an available sentencing option. Many also feel that in states where the death penalty is on the books, it should be used. When capital

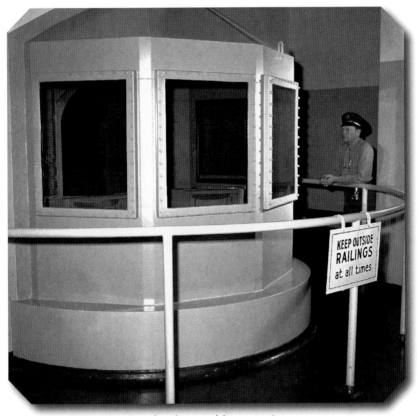

Gas chamber used for executions

punishment is available but not used, many believe society does not benefit from it.

It is important to understand that proponents of the death penalty are not advocating its use lightly. Someone will die as a result of the death penalty. Proponents acknowledge that not every

"The mistaken release of guilty murderers should be of far greater concern than the speculative and heretofore nonexistent risk of the mistaken execution of an innocent person."[5]
—*Paul G. Cassell, Associate Professor of Law, Utah*

crime warrants the death penalty and not every person who causes someone's death deserves to be executed. But they do believe there are cases in which the death penalty is the best—and the right—form of punishment. In those cases, proponents of the death penalty want to ensure that there is no question of an error that might cause either the verdict or the punishment to be overturned.

Family members mourn the loss of Earl Jordon,
the victim of a brutal murder.

Christopher Simmons received the death sentence at age 17.

SPECIAL CONSIDERATIONS

No matter what side of the death penalty issue one is on, there are cases and defendants for which a pro or con stance is not quite as clear-cut as it is in other cases. Whether the issue is about who committed the crime or what crime was

committed, these instances can cause
a reexamination of one's position.

THE DEATH PENALTY AND YOUTH

By late 1987, Western nations
had halted executions for individuals
under the age of 18, except for the
United States. The following year,
the U.S. Supreme Court heard the
case of *Thompson v. Oklahoma*. In 1983,
15-year-old William Thompson
participated in an especially brutal
murder. According to Oklahoma law,
Thompson was a juvenile; the district
attorney successfully petitioned the
court to have him tried as an adult.
Thompson was found guilty and
sentenced to death.

Thompson's case made its
way through the appeals process.
Thompson's attorneys were joined by
organizations such as the American
Bar Association (ABA), Amnesty
International, and the Child Welfare
League of America. They argued

The Youngest

The youngest person to be executed in the United States in the twentieth century was George Stinney, who was 14 years old when executed in 1944. Stinney, an African American, was found guilty of murdering two white girls, ages eight and eleven, in South Carolina.

State law at the time called for anyone over the age of 14 to be tried as an adult. The trial lasted for one afternoon. After a ten-minute deliberation, the all-white jury returned with a guilty verdict. Less than three months after the murders, Stinney was electrocuted.

Later investigations have cast doubt on Stinney's guilt. The girls were struck with a heavy railroad spike, and Stinney could not have lifted it by himself.

that Thompson was too young to face execution. They contended that to do so would be in violation of the cruel and unusual punishment provision of the Eighth Amendment of the U.S. Constitution. When the case reached the U.S. Supreme Court, the justices agreed in a 5–3 vote that it was unconstitutional to execute the 15-year-old.

The next attempt to change the age for which the death penalty can be imposed occurred in 1989. In *Stanford v. Kentucky*, the U.S. Supreme Court was asked to hear the case of Kenneth Stanford. At the age of 17, Stanford killed a man. Tried as an adult, Stanford was found guilty and received the death sentence. Like the defendant in *Thompson v. Oklahoma*, Stanford's case was appealed on the basis that he should not have been tried as an adult and, therefore, he was put in jeopardy of receiving the death penalty. This time, however, the Court rejected the arguments and refused to overturn the conviction. When attempts were made to resubmit the case before the Court in 2002, the majority of the justices voted not to revisit the case.

In 1993, 17-year-old Christopher Simmons murdered a woman in Missouri. Tried as an adult, Simmons was found guilty and sentenced to death. Simmons's defense appealed the ruling, arguing that it was unconstitutional to give the death sentence to a juvenile. The appeals court agreed. The state appealed to the U.S. Supreme Court, and the case was heard in 2004.

On March 1, 2005, the Court's decision was announced. By a 5–4 vote, the justices agreed with the appeals court. The Court ruled that the execution of someone for a crime committed when younger than 18 years of age was in violation of the Eighth Amendment. As a result of the U.S. Supreme Court ruling, the death sentences of 72 other inmates were set aside because their crimes had been committed when they were under the age of 18. Between 1976 and the Court's 2005 ruling, 22 inmates whose crimes were committed when under the age of 18 had been executed, most of them in Texas.

The Court's decision was made partly in order to more closely align the U.S. judicial system with the rest of the Western world. The justices also cited

The International Covenant on Civil and Political Rights

In 1992, the United States ratified the International Covenant on Civil and Political Rights. One provision of the covenant is that the death penalty not be applied to offenders under the age of 18. However, when the United States ratified the covenant, it reserved the right to apply the death penalty to juveniles.

scientific evidence regarding the maturing brain as a factor influencing its decision. Many studies found that the human brain is not fully mature during an individual's teenage years. While other parts of the human body reach their maturity during the teen years, the brain does not reach its full maturity until age 20. Therefore, it was argued, a teenager does not have the capacity to make fully informed decisions.

The Worldview

The United Nations Human Rights Commission (UNHRC) passed a resolution in 1999 calling for a temporary worldwide halt on executions. Though not calling for its abolition in countries that still carried out executions, the UNHRC called on countries to limit the number of crimes for which a death sentence could be received. The UNHRC also called for an end to the execution of juvenile offenders.

Following the resolution, as of April 2005, 89 countries had removed the death penalty from their laws. European nations have abolished the death penalty, considering it a human rights violation.

Another 29 countries practice abolition although the death penalty remains on the books. Argentina, Bolivia, Brazil, Chile, Cook Islands, El Salvador, Fiji, Greece, Israel, Latvia, and Peru restrict the use of the death penalty to only the most heinous crimes.

Countries that still use the death penalty include: Afghanistan, the Bahamas, Belize, China, Ghana, Iran, Iraq, North and South Korea, Libya, Syria, Uganda, the United States, and Vietnam. In 2006, 1,591 executions took place. Of the 76 countries that still execute criminals, just six countries carried out 91 percent of executions—China, Iran, Pakistan, Iraq, Sudan, and the United States.

THE DEATH PENALTY AND THE MENTALLY HANDICAPPED

Early on the morning of August 16, 1996, Daryl

Atkins and an accomplice kidnapped a man from a convenience store in Virginia. When the pair discovered that their victim only had $60, they drove him to an automated teller machine (ATM), where they made him withdraw more money. With $260 from the kidnapping, they drove the victim to an isolated area and shot him eight times.

There was no question as to the pair's guilt; they had been caught on the ATM's surveillance camera. Atkins's descriptions of the events varied almost every time he told the story. Law enforcement personnel and the prosecuting attorney made a deal with Atkins's accomplice: in return for his testimony against Atkins, the accomplice would receive a life sentence and avoid the death penalty.

Based on the accomplice's testimony and other evidence, a jury found Atkins guilty of capital murder, which meant that he was eligible for the death penalty. During the penalty phase, the defense presented his school transcripts and the results of an intelligence quotient (IQ) test. His grades showed that he had been a poor student. He had never lived on his own or held a regular job. The IQ test put his score at 59, which is considered mildly mentally handicapped. Atkins was sentenced to death.

The U.S. Supreme Court agreed to hear the case during its appeal. In 1989, in *Penry v. Lynaugh* the Court had ruled that it was permissible to execute individuals who were mentally handicapped. At the time of the ruling, only two states had prohibited the execution of individuals who were diagnosed as being mentally handicapped. The Court ruled that there was not an established trend that such a practice was wrong.

By 2002, when the Court heard the *Atkins* case, 21 states did not allow the execution of mentally handicapped individuals. These states had determined that executing someone who was mentally handicapped was cruel and unusual punishment. The Court agreed: if it is determined that an individual is mentally handicapped, that person is not eligible for the death penalty.

"In many, but not all states, the defendant cannot be held responsible if he reacted to an 'irresistible impulse' or is incapable for acting responsibly by reason of mental or emotional disability. Many people with mental disabilities, however, are not legally insane. Some persons with mental disabilities have been found legally capable of resisting impulses and acting responsibly."[1]

—UN Commission on Human Rights

BROADENING THE RANGE

State statutes also allow the death sentence for crimes other than murder. The following crimes can also bring the death penalty:

- ❖ Treason: Arkansas, California, Colorado, Georgia, Illinois, Louisiana, Mississippi, Missouri, Washington, and the federal government

- ❖ Aggravated kidnapping: Colorado, Idaho, Illinois, Missouri, and Montana

- ❖ Child rape: Florida, Louisiana, Montana, Oklahoma, and South Carolina

- ❖ Drug trafficking: Florida, Missouri, and the federal government

- ❖ Aircraft hijacking: Georgia and Mississippi

- ❖ Placing a bomb near a bus terminal: Missouri

- ❖ Espionage: New Mexico

- ❖ Aggravated assault by incarcerated, persistent felons, or murderers: Montana.

Sexual Offenders

Opponents of the death penalty agree that something has to be done to prevent sexual offenders from repeating their crimes. But they believe there are other options— longer prison terms, release to a mental hospital, or chemical castration.

Despite the fact that the death penalty is technically a sentencing option for those crimes, most executions are performed only for aggravated murder. The constitutionality of these state statues is highly suspect.

However, in some cases the death penalty is being broadened to include repeat sexual offenders. In 2006, South Carolina Governor Mark Sanford signed Jessie's Law into effect. The law, named after Jessica Lunsford, the victim of a brutal kidnapping and murder, allows the execution of repeat sexual offenders who are convicted of raping children under the age of 11. ⌐

Florida Governor Jeb Bush signs a bill to broaden the penalties for sexual crimes against children.

The Nebraska State Penitentiary houses executions.

THE FUTURE

he criminal justice system is designed to protect the people in a society and punish criminals. However, people differ in opinions on how society is to punish individuals who break laws and threaten public safety. The issue of life and death is black and white, and a compromise in this issue will never be made. In recent years, it appears that U.S. citizens and state legislators have shifted their attitudes regarding the death penalty by favoring life imprisonment sentences.

THE TREND

Although the death penalty continues to have strong support, alternative life sentences are also gaining in support. For example, in 2007, legislatures in Maryland and New Mexico had the opportunity to vote on repealing the death penalty; these bills passed in the Houses of both states but failed by one vote in the Senates. A New Jersey commission studying the use of the death penalty in that state has recommended that it be abolished.

Polls conducted in Maryland, Kansas, and Pennsylvania reflected changing attitudes toward the death penalty in those states. When asked if life without parole was an acceptable alternative to the death penalty for murder, more than 60 percent of those responding said yes. That is approximately 20 percent more than when the question was asked six years ago. In Kansas and Pennsylvania the public favors a sentence of life without parole.

Life in Prison

Without the death penalty, the primary punishment for convicted murderers and other dangerous criminals would be life imprisonment. In most states, when an inmate receives a sentence of life in prison, parole is not possible. Life without parole keeps offenders out of society for the remainder of their lives.

In some cases, an inmate's sentence is commuted to a certain number of years or he or she is awarded time off for good behavior and never receives a true life sentence. However,

Crimes of the Century

In 1924, a crime occurred that captured the country's attention. It was the murder of a Chicago boy, Bobby Franks, by Nathan Leopold (age 19) and Richard Loeb (age 18).

Clarence Darrow defended the boys. His closing argument reads in part:

I sometimes wonder if I am dreaming. If in the first quarter of the twentieth century there has come back into the hearts of men the hate and feeling and the lust for blood which possesses the primitive savage of barbarous lands. What do they want? ... Is there any reason why this great public should be regaled by a hanging? I cannot understand it, Your Honor. It would be past belief, excepting that to the four corners of the earth the news of this weird act has been carried and men have been stirred, and the primitive has come back ... men have been controlled by feelings and passions and hatred which should have died centuries ago.

If these two boys die on the scaffold ... the details of this will be spread over the world ... Will it make men better or make men worse?[1]

The defendants received prison time.

there has been an increasing trend in the prison population: its inmates are getting older. Individuals who have been sentenced to life imprisonment without parole are serving their entire sentences. According to the authors of *The Meaning of Life: Long Prison Sentences in Context*, the Georgia Board of Pardons and Paroles reported in 1998 that more lifers had died in prison that year than were paroled. They had truly served a life sentence.

Of all of the inmates serving life sentences in prison in 2004, one in four was sentenced to life without parole. Six states—Illinois, Iowa, Louisiana, Maine, Pennsylvania, and South Dakota—do not offer life sentencing with the possibility of parole. In these states, a life sentence is always without a parole option.

What Next?

Even if a shift is made that favors life without parole over the

Are Life and Life without Parole Sentences Ineffective?

In 2006, David McGuinn, a corrections officer at the Maryland House of Corrections, was killed when two inmates stabbed him. Lamarr C. Harris was serving a triple life sentence for a double murder in 1989. The other perpetrator, Lee E. Stephens, was incarcerated on a life plus 15 years sentence for murdering a man in 1997. A spokesperson for the state's attorney's office indicated that when there is no death penalty, there is nothing to prevent lifers from killing other inmates and corrections staff.

Prison cellblock hallway

death penalty or if the death penalty is abolished completely, the debate over its use will not be over. Not everyone agrees that life without parole is a better sentencing alternative than the death penalty. Those who favor the death penalty feel that life sentencing is too expensive and that anything short of the death penalty does not bring justice to the victim. They also argue that the deterrent factor is lost when there is no death penalty. An inmate has nothing to lose from killing another inmate or correctional officer, for example, if they are already serving a life sentence. To proponents of the death penalty, a lifetime behind bars does not provide all of the benefits that come with execution.

The United States is an open society that welcomes debate. In fact, the country thrives on it. The death penalty has been debated for decades and most likely, the debate will continue. Proponents and opponents search for the best method of protecting society, punishing criminals, deterring those who contemplate committing a criminal act, and bringing justice to the victims of serious crimes.

For proponents of capital punishment, the death penalty provides the answer to all of those issues—once and for all. Opponents of the death penalty see it another way; they do not feel the death penalty is effective and believe that its use is immoral.

Death Row Inmates

According to the U.S. Department of Justice, as of December 31, 2005, among death row inmates for whom information was available:

• Almost two in three had a prior felony conviction.
• One in 12 had a prior homicide conviction.
• The youngest person on death row was 20 years old.
• The oldest person on death row was 90 years old.

In the debate over the death penalty, only one thing is certain—capital punishment means the difference between life and death. The death penalty is a permanent form of punishment, and great care must be taken when making decisions regarding its use. ⌐

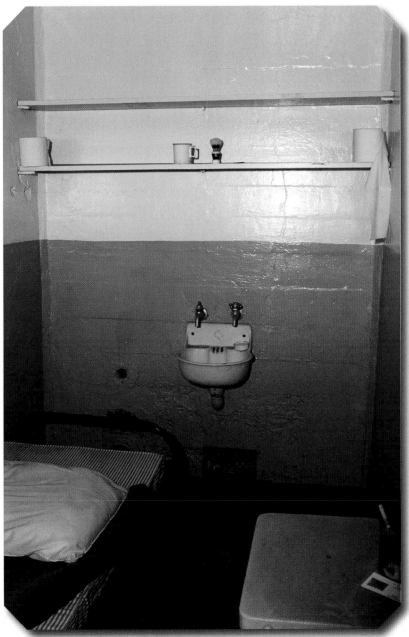

Prison cell

TIMELINE

1608	1632	1848
Captain George Kendall is executed in Virginia for being a spy; he is the first person executed in America.	Jane Champion becomes the first woman executed in America.	Acclaimed author Victor Hugo appeals to France's Constituent Assembly to abolish the death penalty.

1972	1973	1976
On June 29, the U.S. Supreme Court strikes down most elements of the death penalty in its ruling of *Furman v. Georgia.*	A study by Isaac Ehrlich concludes that for every execution, seven lives are saved.	The U.S. Supreme Court ruling on July 2, in *Gregg v. Georgia,* opens the door to resumption of executions.

1924

On February 8, Gee Jon becomes the first person executed by lethal gas.

1936

The last public execution occurs in Owensboro, Kentucky, on August 14.

1968

On June 3, the U.S. Supreme Court rules against a law requiring juries to determine sentencing in death penalty cases.

1977

On June 29, the U.S. Supreme Court rules against using the death sentence for a crime that does not include someone's death.

1986

The U.S. Supreme Court rules on April 30, that attorneys cannot use peremptory challenges to create a one-color jury.

1988

The U.S. Supreme Court rules on June 29 that it is unconstitutional to execute anyone under the age of 16.

TIMELINE

1989	1992	1998

The U.S. Supreme Court rules on June 26 that it is permissible to execute individuals who are mentally handicapped.

The Innocence Project is established to use DNA evidence to help free falsely convicted inmates.

Karla Faye Tucker is executed in Texas on February 3.

2002	2002	2004

The U.S. Supreme Court rules on June 20 that it is unconstitutional to execute a mentally handicapped person.

New Mexico Governor Gary Johnson declares his state's death penalty unfair and open to the execution of innocent people.

New York's death penalty is ruled unconstitutional.

1999	2000	2002
The American Bar Association urges a halt to executions.	Illinois Governor George Ryan places a moratorium on that state's executions.	Maryland Governor Paris Glendening places a hold on executions.

2005	2006	2007
On March 1, the U.S. Supreme Court rules against executions for those whose crimes were committed when they were under the age of 18.	Jessie's Law is established.	The U.S. Supreme Court agrees to hear arguments against the use of lethal injections.

ESSENTIAL FACTS

At Issue

Opposed

❖ The death penalty does not prevent crime.

❖ It costs more to execute an inmate than to keep an inmate incarcerated for life.

❖ Most major religions are opposed to the death penalty.

❖ The death penalty is doled out unfairly.

❖ The death penalty does not bring closure to a victim's family; it only makes more victims.

In Favor

❖ The death penalty acts as a deterrent to those contemplating a criminal act.

❖ The use of the death penalty can be traced throughout the Bible; most holy books of other religions allow for its use.

❖ Executing a murderer shows victims' families that their loved ones' lives did truly have value.

❖ The death penalty prevents criminals from becoming repeat offenders or committing crimes that progressively become more serious.

❖ Some crimes are so heinous that death is the only possible sentence.

Critical Dates

1608
The death penalty was first carried out in the American colonies.

June 29, 1972
In *Furman v. Georgia*, the U.S. Supreme Court struck down most elements of the death penalty.

1973
A study by Isaac Ehrlich concluded that for every execution, seven lives are saved.

July 2, 1976
In *Gregg v. Georgia* the U.S. Supreme Court's ruling opened the door to resumption of executions.

June 29, 1977
In *Coker*, the U.S. Supreme Court ruled that using the death sentence for a crime that does not include someone's death was unconstitutional.

June 29, 1988
The U.S. Supreme Court ruled it unconstitutional to execute anyone found guilty of committing a crime under the age of 16.

June 26, 1989
The U.S. Supreme Court ruled it permissible to execute mentally handicapped individuals.

June 20, 2002
The U.S. Supreme Court ruled it unconstitutional to execute mentally handicapped individuals.

March 1, 2005
The U.S. Supreme Court ruled it unconstitutional to execute individuals for crimes committed when they were under the age of 18.

Quotes

"Look, examine, reflect. You hold capital punishment up as an example. Why? Because of what it teaches. And just what is it that you wish to teach by means of this example? That thou shalt not kill. And how do you teach that 'thou shalt not kill'? By killing."
—*Victor Hugo*

"It is by exacting the highest penalty for the taking of human life that we affirm the highest value of human life."—*Edward Koch*

ADDITIONAL RESOURCES

SELECT BIBLIOGRAPHY

Banner, Stuart. *The Death Penalty: An American History*. Cambridge, MA: Harvard UP, 2002.

Bedau, Hugo, and Paul Cassell, eds. *Debating the Death Penalty: Should America Have Capital Punishment? The Experts from Both Sides Make Their Case*. New York: Oxford UP, 2004.

Cheever, Joan M. *Back from the Dead*. Chichester, West Sussex, UK: John Wiley, 2006.

Death Penalty Information Center. <http://www.deathpenaltyinfo. org>.

Kurtis, Bill. *The Death Penalty on Trial: Crisis in American Justice*. New York: PublicAffairs, 2007.

Rideau, Wilbert, and Ron Wikberg. *Life Sentences: Rage and Survival Behind Bars*. New York: Random House, 1992.

FURTHER READING

Espejo, Roman. *Does Capital Punishment Deter Crime*. Farmington Hills, MI: Greenhaven Press, 2002.

Fisanick, Christina. *The Ethics of Capital Punishment*. Farmington Hills, MI: Greenhaven Press, 2004.

Gottfried, Ted. *Death Penalty*. Minneapolis, MN: Twenty-First Century Books, 2002.

Henningfeld, Diane Andrews, ed. *The Death Penalty*. Farmington Hills, MI: Greenhaven, 2006.

Web Links

To learn more about the death penalty, visit ABDO Publishing Company on the World Wide Web at **www.abdopublishing.com.** Web sites about the death penalty are featured on our Book Links page. These links are routinely monitored and updated to provide the most current information available.

For More Information

For more information on this subject, contact or visit the following organizations.

American Civil Liberties Union
125 Broad Street, 18th Floor
New York, NY 10004
http://www.aclu.com/
The American Civil Liberties Union opposes the death penalty. Contact them for information or to support movements to abolish the death penalty.

The Death Penalty Information Center
1101 Vermont Avenue NW, Suite 701
Washington, DC 20005
http://www.deathpenaltyinfo.org/
The Death Penalty Information Center provides recent studies, statistics, and general information on the death penalty.

U.S. Supreme Court
Public Information Officer
Supreme Court of the United States
One First Street NE
Washington, DC 20543
http://www.supremecourtus.gov/
The U.S. Supreme Court has upheld the use of the death penalty. Contact them for information on court decisions.

GLOSSARY

attorney general
> The chief legal adviser of a state or a country.

capital crime
> A crime that is punishable by the death penalty.

civil rights
> Rights that are guaranteed to all citizens of a society.

closure
> A sense of finality and coming to terms with an experience.

commute
> To reduce the severity of a penalty.

criminologist
> A researcher who studies the sociology of crime, criminals, and punishment.

cyanide
> A poisonous salt.

death row
> An area within a correctional facility where inmates sentenced to death are housed.

defendant
> Someone required to answer criminal or civil charges in court.

deterrent
> Something that discourages someone from taking a particular action.

DNA
> Deoxyribonucleic acid; the substance that carries an organism's genetic information.

felony
> A serious crime that is punished severely.

heinous
> Shockingly evil or wicked.

incarcerate
> To place someone in a correctional facility.

mandatory
> Required to be complied with.

moratorium
> A formally agreed period during which a specific activity is halted.

parameter
> A circumstance that restricts how something is done or what can be done.

pardon
> To officially release someone guilty of a crime or wrongdoing from facing punishment.

parole
> The early release of an inmate with certain conditions attached.

premeditate
> To plan something before taking action.

provision
> A preparatory step taken to meet an expected need.

psychopath
> A term for someone with a personality disorder marked by antisocial thought and behavior.

public defender
> An attorney assigned to represent defendants who cannot afford their own attorney.

rehabilitation
> Training, therapy, or other help given to someone that will enable the individual to lead a healthy and productive life.

stereotype
> A widely held and oversimplified idea of something.

treason
> Violation of the allegiance owed by an individual to his or her own country.

unconstitutional
> Forbidden by the U.S. Constitution.

Source Notes

Chapter 1. The Death Penalty: A Solution?
1. The United States Constitution. The U.S. Constitution Online. 2 Oct. 2007 <http://www.usconstitution.net/const.html>
2. *Furman v. Georgia* Case Summary. ACLU.org. 2 Oct. 2007. <www.acluprocon.org/SupCtCases/225Furman.html>.
3. The United States Constitution. The U.S. Constitution Online. 2 Oct. 2007 <http://www.usconstitution.net/const.html>
4. *Furman v. Georgia*. "U.S. Supreme Court Decided June 29, 1972". 2 Oct. 2007 <www.law.umkc.edu/faculty/projects/ftrials/conlaw/furman.html>.
5. Ibid.

Chapter 2. Death Penalty Basics
None.

Chapter 3. Overview of the Controversy
1. Victor Hugo. Quoted on "Death Penalty News & Updates." 2 Oct. 2007 <http://people.smu.edu/peri>.
2. "Arguments For and Against the Death Penalty." Death Penalty Information Center. 2 Oct. 2007 <deathpenaltyinfo.msu.edu/c/about/arguments/argument1b.htm>.
3. Ibid.

Chapter 4. Religion and Death Penalty Proponents
1. The United States Constitution. The U.S. Constitution Online. 2 Oct. 2007. <http://www.usconstitution.net/const.html>
2. *The Holy Bible*. King James version. Genesis 9. 6. Electronic Text Center. University of Virginia Library. 2 Oct. 2007 <http://etext.virginia.edu/etcbin/toccer-new2?id=KjvGene.sgm&images=images/modeng&data=/texts/english/modeng/parsed&tag=public&part=9&division=div1>.

Chapter 5. Religion and Death Penalty Opponents

1. *The Holy Bible*. King James version. Genesis 4. 11–15. Electronic Text Center. University of Virginia Library. 2 Oct. 2007 <http://etext.virginia.edu/etcbin/toccer-new2?id=KjvGene. sgm&images=images/modeng&data=/texts/english/modeng/parsed &tag=public&part=9&division=div1>.

2. Aryeh Kaplan. *Handbook of Jewish Thought, vol. II.* Brooklyn, NY: Moznaim, 1992. 170–171.

3. Moses Maimonides. *The Commandments*. Charles B. Chavel, trans. Brooklyn, NY: Soncino Press, 1984. 269–271.

4. "The Death Penalty and Jewish Values." The Jewish Perspective. *Religious Action Center of Reform Judaism*. 2 Oct. 2007 <http://rac.org/ Articles/index.cfm?id=1665&pge_prg_id=8089&pge_id=2396 >.

Chapter 6. Objections to the Death Penalty

1. Stereotypically "Black-Looking" Criminals More Likely to Get Death Sentence, Researchers Find." *Diverse Issues in Higher Education*. 1 June 2006. <www.diverseeducation.com/artman/publish/ article_5947.shtml>.

2. Ibid.

3. Stephen B. Bright. "Why the United States Will Join the Rest of the World in Abandoning Capital Punishment." In Hugo Bedau and Paul Cassell, eds. *Debating the Death Penalty: Should America Have Capital Punishment*. New York: Oxford UP, 2004. 167.

4. "Hippocratic Oath—Modern Version." *Nova Online*. 2 Oct. 2007 <www.pbs.org/wgbh/nova/doctors/oath_modern.html>.

Source Notes continued

Chapter 7. Support for the Death Penalty

1. Edward Koch. Quoted on Religious Tolerance. *The Ontario Consultants on Religious Tolerance.* 2 Oct. 2007 <http://www.religioustolerance.org/executb.htm>.

2. Ernest van den Haag. "The Ultimate Punishment: A Defense." *PBS.org.* 2 Oct. 2007 <http://www.pbs.org/wgbh/pages/frontline/angel/procon/haagarticle.html>.

3. "Arguments For and Against the Death Penalty." *Death Penalty Information Center.* 2 Oct. 2007 <deathpenaltyinfo.msu.edu>.

4. Gregory Kane. "To murder victims' families, executing killers is justice". Baltimore Sun, 5 Feb. 2003. <www.baltimoresun.com/news/local/bal-md.kane05feb05,1,41347>.

5. Paul G. Cassell. "Statement of Paul G. Cassell Associate Professor of Law University of Utah College of Law Before the Committee on the Judiciary United States House of Representatives Subcommittee on Civil and Constitutional Rights Concerning Claims of Innocence in Capital Cases on July 23, 1993," 2 Oct. 2007. <http://www.carmical.net/resources/TESthousehearing.htm>.

Chapter 8. Special Considerations
1. "The Question of the Death Penalty." UN Commission on Human Rights. 2 Oct. 2007 <http://www.unhchr.ch>.

Chapter 9. The Future
1. Clarence Darrow. "Closing Argument: *The State of Illinois v. Nathan Leopold & Richard Loeb.*" August 22, 1924. 2 Oct. 2007 <http://www.umkc.edu/faculty/projects/ftrials/sweet/Darrowsumm1.html>.

Index

ABOUT THE AUTHOR

Ida Walker is the author of several nonfiction books for middle-grade and young-adult readers. Her special interest is civil rights and the history of their development in the United States. She has visited many of the locations of the memorable events of the civil rights movement of the late 1950s and 1960s. She lives in New York.

PHOTO CREDITS

Mark Foley/AP Images, cover, 3; AP Images, 6, 15, 51, 96, 98 (top); Jupiterimages/AP Images, 16, 25, 56, 61, 92, 95; Jack Smith/AP Images, 26, 67, 98 (bottom); Scott Osborne/AP Images, 32; Red Line Editorial/Nicole Brecke, 34; Charles Bennett/AP Images, 37, 65; George Osodi/AP Images, 38; Steve Miller/AP Images, 41; Karen Tam/AP Images, 42; Don Wright/AP Images, 47; Plinio Lepri/AP Images, 48; Hasan Sarbakhshian/AP Images, 55; Chris O'Meara/AP Images, 68, 99; Clarence Hamm/AP Images, 75, 97; Larry McCarmack/AP Images, 77; Missouri Department of Corrections/AP Images, 78; Phil Coale/AP Images, 87; Daniel Luedert/AP Images, 88.